The Future of Eucharist

How a new self-awareness
among Catholics is changing
the way they believe and worship.

by
Bernard Cooke

PAULIST PRESS
New York • Mahwah, N.J.

Cover design by Kathy McKeen.

Portions of this book appeared previously as an article in *The National Catholic Reporter.*

Library of Congress Cataloging-in-Publication Data

Cooke, Bernard J.
    The future of Eucharist : how a new self-awareness among Catholics is changing the way they believe and worship / by Bernard Cooke.
        p.   cm.
    ISBN 0-8091-3697-X (alk. paper)
    1. Mass. 2. Catholic Church—United States—Liturgy. 3. Catholic Church—United States—Liturgy. 4. United States—Church history—20th century. I. Title.
    BX2230.5.C66 1997
    264'.02036—dc20   96-32560
                                                                                           CIP

Published by Paulist Press
997 Macarthur Boulevard
Mahwah, New Jersey 07430

Printed and bound in the
United States of America

1

The Roots of Change

Recent decades have seen a rapid up-and-down in Catholics' expectations about the future of eucharist. Up to the Second Vatican Council there were moves toward liturgical revision, but few people were aware of them and even fewer were interested. The Mass was the Mass, one was expected to attend each Sunday under pain of sin, and that was that. The nascent liturgical movement was viewed with distrust or disinterest by most, laity and clergy alike. Then a somewhat hesitant approval was given by the Papal encyclical *Mediator Dei* (1947). Much more importantly, the first major decree of Vatican II proposed a basic renewal of the church's liturgies and the move to a new era of eucharistic life was initiated. With little preparatory or even follow-up explanation given to people, the changes in eucharistic celebration came as a surprise to most Catholics, were feared and even rejected by some, but for the most part were accepted and welcomed.

Today, however, the new hopes for a revitalized eucharistic celebration in the church are threatened by a rapidly diminishing number of ordained presiders. As fewer and fewer parishes have their own resident eucharistic leader, what is the future for celebration of eucharist on a regular basis? I will discuss this question later and suggest that the threat may not be as serious as it appears. Still, there is no question but what the decline in "vocations" raises basic questions about the nature and frequency of eucharistic activity in the future.

A New Context of Christian Worship

Much of the writing and speaking on the future of Catholic liturgy has tended to stress the crisis character of today's situation, to worry that a decline in the eucharistic spirituality which has characterized the Catholic tradition is almost inevitable for countries in Europe and the Americas. Such predictions of doom are premature. Indeed, the future of eucharist is exciting; it could turn out to be a period of unprecedented liturgical development, for at no time in the church's history has there been greater potential for development.

This not to say that there is no risk. Change is always risky and noticeable changes have occurred in the celebration of eucharist since the council, changes that have been unsettling for many because little, if any, explanation has been given to people by their pastors. There is also no doubt that the activity of the ordained is of critical importance as we move into what will certainly be a new context of Christian worship—and so concern about the availability of ordained presiders is clearly justified. But it is at least possible that the deeper changes that helped bring about official modification of liturgical forms and the diversity of demographic contexts for eucharistic celebration point to betterment rather than decline.

The promise of a better future for eucharist springs

from the deeper changes that have been happening to liturgical celebration in recent decades. These changes, which have to do with the inner *awareness and attitudes* of Catholics as they gather for eucharist, have already launched us on a new and exciting path. What is changing is the very reality of Christian faith, not a rejection of the basic faith that has animated Christians for two millennia but a more mature understanding of and commitment to that faith. This inevitably means a basic shift in Catholic participation in the liturgy, because the ritual of eucharist is the primary symbol that expresses faith and creates Christian community.

How has participation shifted? First of all, Vatican II insisted that Catholics gathered for eucharist should understand what is happening so that they can consciously share in the enactment of the ritual. In the council's own words:

> The church earnestly desires that Christ's faithful, when present at this mystery of faith, should not be there as strangers or silent spectators. On the contrary, through a good understanding of the rites and prayers they should take part in the sacred action, conscious of what they are doing, with devotion and full collaboration." (#48)

This statement is a 180-degree turn of immense importance. Instead of "receiving sacraments," "attending Mass," "hearing Mass"—i.e. simply being there and "watching Father do his thing"—Catholics are increasingly aware that they along with the ordained presider are the *doers* of the liturgical action. Participation in the liturgy has come to mean much more than attentively observing what is taking place at the altar and from time to time saying "Amen." Laywomen and men are in many places taking roles intrinsic to the liturgical action, such as proclaiming the biblical texts or acting as eucharistic ministers—something unheard of less than a half century ago. Robert McClory's reports (in the *National Catholic Reporter*) on sacramental practice in the U.S. bear witness to the vitality of eucharist in those communities where pastor and people are aware of and practicing this new conjoined liturgical activity. In these centers of vitality, the *experience* of eucharist has changed. Not only is the eucharist able to influence the meaning of people's lives, the meaning of their lives becomes part of the awareness of eucharist. Yes, change has occurred since the council, much of it very positive, and change that promises an even brighter future. Yes, we have scarcely scratched the surface in the effort to follow through on the liturgical principles enunciated by Vatican II. Yes, danger seems to threaten because of the shrinking number of the ordained, but perhaps this threat is not as great as it seems. Perhaps the greater threat is that we will grow apathetic and cease efforts to implement the liturgical principles laid down by Vatican II.

The observable aspects of liturgical change are only the tip of the iceberg. To say this is not to minimize the importance of the changes that followed the council. To have put the ritual in the language of the people was indispensable if the bulk of Catholics were to understand and actively participate—though we have discovered that use of the vernacular has not by itself created such understanding and participation. Turning the altar around so that the presider now faces the community brought about a new experience of relation between presider and people that is very different from the old days when Father spoke Latin to a wall with his back turned to the congregation. In that former situation it was almost impossible to have the ritual symbolize a family gathered around a table for a sacred meal. Scholars of ritual point out how the change in what is seen and heard has great influence on the character and location of power in a group—which is another way of saying that our ecclesiology is subtly but profoundly altered by the way the eucharist is celebrated.

When one reflects on the opposition in some circles to the notion of receiving communion in the hand when it was first proposed, or the way altar boys were drilled never to let their bare hand touch an empty ciborium when they brought it to the sacristy after Mass, it's truly amazing to realize that lay women and men distributing communion is now considered commonplace. This represents an invasion of the sacred by "unconsecrated" laity that touches implicitly the whole power-base of the ordained clergy. While less far-reaching in its implications, the introduction of altar girls has contributed in its own way to a shift in the symbolic message of the ritual action. One must be careful not to undersell the powerful message being sent by these postconciliar liturgical changes. Still, the radical shifts—"radical" in the basic meaning of that term because they are the "roots" of the more visible changes—go much further and are bound to lead to as yet unimagined liturgical revision.

The Inner Awareness of Catholics

These more radical changes, as we said, are occurring in the inner awareness of Catholics at eucharist. They have to do with the presuppositions Catholics bring to the celebration of eucharist, the understandings and attitudes and worldview and commitment that shape the very reality of their eucharistic activity. Because by its very nature eucharist reflects the life of the people, because it is the primary profession of people's Christian faith and of their relation to God, eucharist points to the deeper shifts that are taking place in people's understandings and choices and activity. Eucharistic change translates in symbol the seismic shifts occurring in the whole of Christianity. At the heart of the liturgical action of eucharist, beneath the observable activity of priest and people, lie the inner awareness and commitment and openness to God's saving activity that are the reality of faith and hope and love. It is these inner elements of people's liturgical celebration that are undergoing fundamental change; and it is this deeper change that will continue to alter—I believe very positively—the character of Christianity as a eucharistic community.

Eucharist is a ritual action. Like any ritual is has power to shape, strengthen, or transform the group of people involved in the ritual. But like any ritual, its power, indeed its very reality, depends upon the people knowing what they are doing and accepting the implications of what the ritual says. To take a homely example, suppose a group of people from Zambia in Africa were brought together and *without understanding the words* memorized the pledge recited by new U.S. citizens on the day they receive citizenship. Externally, as they speak the words aloud, the action may seem exactly like that performed by new citizens, yet no one would believe the Zambians were accepting U.S. citizenship and its responsibilities. Roughly parallel, the fact that Catholics now know better what is being said in the liturgy means that the action has undergone considerable change, and further change will come as their understanding and commitment grow.

The Force of Inculturation

Without anticipating the material of subsequent chapters, let me mention just one element of change to suggest the extent to which current change is reaching. For centuries the forms of eucharistic celebration have been imposed on local communities throughout the world from one center, Rome. The language used and all the details of the ritual were decided at the Vatican, incorporated in the *Missale Romanum* and expected to be carried out with religious obedience in every part of the globe. However, we have come to learn that, to be effective, ritual—and the eucharist is ritual—must emerge from the community that celebrates it. So while guidance from Rome should be cherished, we cannot expect a Roman formulary as such to express and shape the faith and life of communities in all the various portions of the world. How we move away from homogeneity and at the same time reinforce eucharistic unity is something we must learn. Obviously we must combine fearless caution with responsible creativity, something we could not do if the Spirit of God were not active in our midst.

Some aspects of this inner change are already observable in communities where the exhortations of Vatican II's *Constitution on the Sacred Liturgy* have been taken to heart.

Under dedicated and informed pastoral leadership many parishes have been animated as true communities of faith and discipleship, some even renaming themselves as "the *community* of such-and-such" to make the point. Serious efforts are being made to come to a better understanding of the bible, the traditional beliefs of Christianity, and the present life of the church. There is a noticeable increase in concern for the sick and disabled. Perhaps most tellingly, there is a genuine and effective dedication to working for social justice. And all this finds expression and nurture in the community's eucharistic celebrations.

Subsequent chapters will talk about some of these deeper changes in the beliefs and lives of Catholics which, though perhaps scarcely noticed, have already had immense influence and will most likely impact sacramental liturgies even more in the future. Before going on to detail those, however, one or two preliminary remarks need to be made.

First of all, our concern about Catholic life in North America is clearly important, for us who live here but also because of the immense impact now and for the immediate future that all things "American" have on the rest of the world; *but* we are not the whole church. As a matter of fact, we, together with Catholics in Europe (what we consider "traditional" Christianity), are rapidly becoming a minority. Our survival as Christians is not equatable with the survival of the church. Much of the future of Christianity and specifically of its worship life lies in what we characterize as the Third World. In places like Africa and Asia, and even in Latin America, the present state and dynamics of eucharistic practice are becoming quite different from what they are in our part of the church.

It is in these other lands that the issue of inculturation which is intrinsic to all liturgical celebration is being recognized and faced in ways far beyond our attempts to make eucharist more relevant for people. Precisely because the dissonance between the cultural world of Rome and that of African or Asian nations is so evident, liturgical modifications become unavoidable. As modification takes place, it will inevitably impact on us also, because underlying their situation and ours are certain fundamental problems of inculturation we all share. Wherever Catholics are, the celebration of eucharist must grow out of culture in order to transform that culture. We in the Euro-American church have not yet found ways of celebrating liturgy that honor the different cultures—Hispanic, Afro-American, youth, women—that exist in our own country. This issue of inculturation is immense. We will not be able to treat it in the short scope of this volume, but we must keep it in mind as the broader context in which our "problems" need to be confronted. We are by no means alone in the task of helping the liturgy of future Christianity to emerge. As a matter of fact we may turn out to be a minor agent of the change that does occur.

Secondly, the following pages will be an exercise in what all of us who have been baptized into a prophetic community are called to do individually and together in community: To read the signs of the times, to discover in these signs the action of God in our day so that we can be the instruments of its implementation. No one of us can claim to have the ultimate reading. Each of us must work to discover and then to share with others, so that out of this shared discourse we may arrive at a more accurate understanding. It is my hope that sharing my views, limited as they necessarily are, will stimulate others to complement and challenge and correct, so that together we may know a bit better where we are going and what needs to be done in order to bring about the reign of God in our day and to celebrate that reign eucharistically.

Some of these signs are subtle and easily escape notice. But others are quite apparent even when we wish they were not there. The presence in power of God's Spirit has been manifested in a number of charismatic developments in the church's life in this century. This is not only a matter of the so-called "charismatic movement" which has taken many forms, some of which have been a profound enrichment of the church's prayer life while others attributed to God's Spirit attitudes that seem contrary to the gospel. Much more far-reaching have been the "miracle" of the Second Vatican Council, the ecumenical movement that came in reaction to Nazism, or the sprouting of grassroots base communities in Africa and Latin America. Pope John XXIII himself pointed to contemporary women's advance toward equality as one of the principal signs of the times. All of these have already had and will continue to have their impact on Christian celebration of eucharist. If they are evidence of God's Spirit working in our day, they cannot be ignored as guideposts in efforts toward further liturgical renewal.

2

New Understandings of Sin

In the previous chapter we mentioned that the changes in eucharist are not primarily the external modifications that have occurred since Vatican II. Instead, it is the underlying attitudes and understandings that Catholics are now bringing to eucharist that make the reality of liturgy different. Even though the external ceremonies remain the same from Sunday to Sunday or from place to place, no two celebrations are exactly the same because the reality of eucharist is that it is a *human experience*, and how eucharist is experienced depends on the precise group of Catholics who gather, their dispositions on a particular day, their understandings, level of attention and involvement, etc. The actual experience of eucharist is changing for people and will continue to change, because the presuppositions that people bring to eucharist are undergoing basic change.

Though it may have happened quietly, the change in people's understanding of and attitudes toward sin is one of the most influential shifts that has occurred in recent decades. It has affected believers and non-believers alike, for it has altered the cultural outlook we share. As we will see in a moment, this shift has immense implications for eucharistic experience, since the eucharistic liturgy is Christianity's primary sacrament of reconciliation. But first, to better understand the shift that has happened and to put into perspective the present outlook on sin, a quick glance at past centuries may help.

Distrust of Bodiliness

While the earliest decades of Christianity were relatively free from negativity regarding the human body, it was only a short time before the ultra-spiritualism associated with Platonic philosophy began to influence Christian ethical outlooks. Not all went the lengths of Manicheism; still the influence of Neo-Platonism from the third century onward, flowing through Origen and Augustine into the patristic tradition and then through figures like Augustine and Pseudo-Dionysius into medieval thought, did notably increase Christians' distrust of human bodiliness. Sexuality in particular was viewed as a problem, a source of temptation, an obstacle to holiness. Even marital intercourse was looked on with suspicion by many church fathers; sexual relations between spouses were justified only because of the obvious need for procreation, but such marital intercourse was to be engaged in with a minimum of pleasure.

Over the centuries, in large part linked to this negative view of what it means to be human, Christians developed a sense of constant sinfulness. True, there were some "real" Christians who abandoned the world with all its temptations and sin and fled to monasteries or their equivalent. But the bulk of people were left to mire in their sin. Besides, a superficial view of divine providence led people to assume that physical evils like plagues or droughts were God's punishment for this sinfulness, sent by God to lead people to repentance and hopefully to salvation. One needs only to read an account of Europe's reaction to the Black Death or see Ingmar Bergman's *The Seventh Seal* to realize how pervading was this atmosphere of sin and punishment.

We should not stress this gloom to the point of forgetting the positive understandings about divine mercy that did exist, the power attributed to practices like pilgrimages or to prayer to the saints, especially Mary. Yet the stress on sin was there, and it was intrinsic to the theological explanation of salvation and sacraments that emerged. Because the sinfulness of humans was so much stressed, it is not surprising that the principal action of God was seen to be that of forgiving sins. However, a just God could not simply forgive sin. Sin as an offense against God, a disregard for God's laws, needed to be somehow compensated for if justice was to reign. Enter the redeeming action of Jesus which was increasingly viewed as *satisfaction* for human sin. By the Middle Ages the notion of satisfaction had come to dominate the theology of salvation. Anselm of Canterbury, in the twelfth century, was not the first to formulate this theory, but his *Cur deus homo* (Why God became human) had a major influence. Its formulation was quite simple: sin's offense against God was of infinite proportions because of God's infinite majesty, so the redeemer had to be able to do something with *infinite* compensatory power; but the offense had been committed by humans, so a human had to make amends. The result was that only one both human and divine could effect redemption. God with divine pity arranged for such a merciful righting of cosmic justice—God's own Son became human and died for our sins.

Jesus' death on Calvary was interpreted as saving us, because it satisfied divine justice and paid the price for our sins. And since by Anselm's day the eucharist had come to be linked almost exclusively with Jesus' death as the sacrifice that blotted out our offenses, overshadowing the link with resurrection which had been foremost in earliest Christianity, the eucharist itself came to be seen as a sacrificial act connected with Calvary and thereby bringing about forgiveness of sin.

Christians were urged to attend Mass in order that their sins might somehow be washed away by the continuing sacrifice of Christ. It was at Mass that the saving merits of Christ's death would be applied to those present. Christians came to the eucharist as sinners and left as sinners, but now as forgiven sinners. As a matter of fact, actual attendance was not needed; if the eucharistic action was offered for the intention of someone alive or dead, the forgiveness merited by Christ could touch that person's sinfulness "at a distance" and reconcile him or her to God.

To make a long story short, for centuries Christians were dominated, at times obsessed, by their sinfulness. Infants were born with original sin, and while baptism remedied the basic alienation from God that was the inheritance of Adam's sin, there still remained a fundamental inclination to sin. Not surprisingly, this inclination usually led to people's own immoral activity and only the existence of sacramental rituals through which divine mercy could be channeled to them made eternal salvation a realistic hope.

A New View of Sin

This outlook has changed in the past half century or so. What has happened is not a denial of human need for divine mercy, but a considerable shift in the understanding of sin and a consequent lessening of emphasis on forgiveness of sin as the heart of God's relationship to believers. Several influences have brought about this reevaluation of humans and their actions. Christian anthropology has reconsidered the behavioral theories of twentieth-century psychology. Our insight into the dynamics of human motivation and decision-making, especially in the area of sexuality, has clearly modified our understanding of culpability. Moreover, the ordinary failings of individual persons that had occupied center stage in the understanding of sin paled when compared to the massive evil attached to the Spanish Civil War, the extermination of millions of innocent human beings by the Nazi regime, the human suffering attendant upon the Second World War and the brutal political elimination of millions of "enemies" by the Stalinist government in Russia. Christians have not been blinded to the reality of sin, but they have come to put into better perspective the presumed sinfulness of most people.

Another extremely important influence has come into play in recent decades: the careful research into the bible and a resultant clarification of the revelation it reflects. For Christians this has resulted in a better understanding of Jesus, his genuine humanity and teaching. Consequently we came to a more balanced view of the divine action of salvation that occurred in Jesus. It isn't accidental that as attitudes changed toward sin, one of the more influential books on moral teaching, by Bernard Häring, was entitled *The Law of Christ*. Reflection on the New Testament made it clear that

Jesus was certainly aware of sin—even more aware than other humans precisely because of his unique relationship with the loving God whom sin rejects. But it also became clear that God was not a divine judge intent on demanding compensation but one who loved and sought out the sinner. The father of the prodigal in Jesus' parable not only forgave but without redress restored the erring son to full share in the family. In a subtle but effective way, greater acquaintance with the message of the New Testament began to influence attitudes toward sin and toward the eucharist as related to sin.

The Social Dimension of Sin

One of the very healthy insights that came with greater reflection on the gospels was our fresh appreciation of the sins targeted by Jesus in his teaching. While he certainly didn't approve of sexual exploitation or irresponsibility, Jesus' ethical teaching did not concentrate on sexual immorality in the manner that has marked centuries of Christian moral teaching, even up to the present. Jesus' sharpest criticism was directed to dishonesty, particularly the hypocrisy of those in high places. With those considered sinners or apprehended in sexual misconduct he was understanding and gentle at the same time that he told them to turn from their sin. On the positive side, his insistence was on loving concern for others rather than on "purity," though again we must not forget his resonance with the innocence of children.

Without a doubt, dangers lay in this move away from focus on personal sinfulness. The psychological community, which had tended to describe moral culpability as the result of psychological influences of one sort or another, had to be reminded that sin is a reality. Karl Menninger's famous little book drew attention again to the existence and importance of sin; not only does sin exist, he said, but accepting and dealing with culpability when present cannot be ignored in effective psychological therapy. This very sensible and honest admonition by one of the country's leading therapists—while not denying that sin was conditioned by any number of influences—made it clear that sin is a key factor in many persons' psychological problems. Sin when it does exist is a destructive influence in human life. To put it in religious terminology, conversion is often central to psychological healing.

But what did all this have to do with the change in eucharistic celebration? What has happened, I believe, is that people—at least many of them—now come to the eucharist with a different understanding of themselves, a new appreciation of the relationship between themselves and God and new reasons for participating in the eucharistic action. It would be naive to think that a total shift in attitudes has occurred. Many Catholics still need to be convinced that they are good and that very few "grave" sins are committed. The gospel of God's love that confers unbelievable dignity on all humans still needs to be heard. But the fear-filled outlook that played such a prominent place in Christian lives, especially among really believing and dedicated Christians, has retreated in the face of a more accurate view of the God revealed in Jesus and a more balanced understanding of the sources and character of moral evil.

Along with this has come a realization for millions of Catholics that eternal life is not essentially governed by others—namely by church officials. Modern Catholics have not been plagued by the large-scale excommunications of whole populations that took place in medieval centuries, although the displeasure or negative judgment of ordained pastors still seemed to imperil one's relation with God and therefore one's eternal destiny. Persons now are more aware that, though ordained persons may play a special role in God's activity in and through the church, God is not bound by unjustified condemning actions by churchmen.

Not Out of Fear

To put it quite simply, more and more people in our day are coming to eucharist not out of fear but out of a true desire to come closer to the risen Christ and with him to God. Unfortunately, in some cases this has meant that as the fear vanished so did the motivation for attending Mass, and so some have drifted away from participation in eucharist. The obvious response to this development is not to reinstill the fear but to make clear the true reasons for sharing in this central Christian action.

Linked with this movement away from fear, away from stress on the need for satisfaction to be made to God for human sin, away from an unbalanced emphasis on sinfulness and need for a mysterious salvation channeled through those empowered by ordination to forgive sin, has been the shift in christological emphasis from death to resurrection. One has to be careful to assess this accurately. It would be a mistake if Christians underestimated the basic role played by the death of Jesus as a source of salvation. But what do Catholics today think that Jesus actually did to redeem us from sin? How and why did he institute the church and its sacraments—or did he? What part does he play in the ongoing process of saving humans in the course of human history? What is his resurrection all about? These questions are being raised in new form today, and they shape the presuppositions that people bring to their celebration of eucharist. In most cases Catholics are unconscious of it, but inevitably their outlook on these issues deeply influences what eucharist means for them and how they share in the ritual. Central to all this is the relation they feel they have with Jesus; so our next chapter will try to deal with that.

3

The Real Jesus

One of the key presuppositions Christians have always brought to eucharist is their understanding of and attitude toward Jesus of Nazareth. This has never been truer than it is today when knowledge about Jesus is probably more accurate than it has been for almost two millennia. Nothing is more prominent nor more important in contemporary scripture studies than the attempt to recover from the New Testament texts the evidence about Jesus of Nazareth and his ministry. And nothing has more impact on the celebration of the eucharist, precisely because it is at its heart a remembrance of Jesus. Obviously, it is critically important to remember Jesus as he actually was, the real Jesus who was (and still is) God's own Word.

The struggle to obtain as accurate a picture as possible of Jesus has been difficult and contentious—it still is. For centuries it was assumed that one could proceed quite easily from the gospel story of Jesus. The gospels were, after all, accounts of Jesus provided by immediate witnesses. But then, from the eighteenth century onward, scholars undertook critical studies of literary texts, including the scriptures. Gradually official church opposition to using such methods to study the bible was overcome and modern biblical study as we now know it emerged. While Catholic scholars suffered from official reluctance to accept critical study of the scriptures, the opposition of conservative Vatican circles did have the benefit of forcing an *extra careful* appraisal of the latest critical approach to the text.

Recovering the Humanity of Jesus

Careful study has made it clear that the gospels are not simple chronicles of what Jesus was and did—they were not intended to be. Instead, the four gospels are theological explanations of Jesus' mission that were intended for catechesis and ritual, explanations of what is was that God achieved in this Jesus, particularly in his dying and rising. While solidly grounded in, indeed triggered by, the reality of Jesus and his activity, New Testament literature is a reflection on the *meaning* of this man whom they believed to be more than just human. What they thought they knew of him from associating with him in his public ministry was shattered by their experience of him alive and with them after his death. After his resurrection they asked about him, talked about him, thanked God for what had happened in him, felt his presence still with them when they gathered for "the breaking of the bread." From this puzzled pondering both the gospels and the eucharist came to be.

For these earliest Christians there was no question of Jesus' full humanity; that was taken for granted. They had eaten with him, seen him jostled by the crowds seeking healing, saw him sad and fearful as death came to him through the betrayal of one of his own. It was only with the passage of time that insistence on the divine dimension of this Jesus, his identity as God's only Son, came to overshadow his human-ness and subtly undermine his humanity. Early councils of the church that shaped credal statements about Jesus rejected the belief that he was less than "true human," but there continued well into the twentieth century a tendency to see his humanity inflated to ultra-humanity because of its link with divinity.

However for at least the past millennium there has been a growing appreciation of the human Jesus, until in this cen-tury the human reality of Jesus has come to be accepted with-out qualification—so much so that the methodology of christology itself has shifted, with the so-called "christology from below" challenging the dominance of "christology from above" that had prevailed for most of Christian history. Today "the search for the historical Jesus" has become almost obsessive. Book after book tries to outdo its predecessors by speculating about the "real Jesus." Some of these that use careful social scientific analysis to reconstruct the Palestine of Jesus' day mark a real gain in our understanding of what life must have been for Jesus. Others, however, seem more interested in gaining attention by "debunking" Christian claims that Jesus was special.

The Lessons of Jesus' Humanity

This is not the place to assess these recent develop-ments in study of the gospels. Technical arguments about textual methods and historical evidences have relatively little immediate influence on the belief and religious practice of most people. What is impacting people's approach to eucharist is the grassroots acceptance that Jesus was truly human as we are human. While people of faith can accept the traditional belief in Jesus' "divinity," understanding that the unparalleled exposure to that God made Jesus' inner awareness unique, they also believe that he went through the same sequence of experiences that constitutes human life for each of us. He was born as we were, had to grow from infancy to childhood to maturity through a process of learning as we do, had to make choices, had to discover and establish his self-identity though these experiences. If he did not he wasn't truly human, because this is what it means to be human.

More than that, he was very limited. Like the rest of us he had one culture with its mother tongue. He lived at a particular point in history and was exposed to only a fraction of what was occurring at that time. He knew a limited number of people, and he related to them as a Jewish male raised in Galilee. These things were known before but were often accepted with qualification, for there was an assumption that some "superhumaness" must have marked him, since he, Jesus of Nazareth, was the Son of God.

Whether or not the more accurate knowledge of the historical reality of Jesus we now possess is the reason for it, there is no denial that interest in Jesus rather than in the church has become once more the focus of Christians' religious lives. Within a generation a large segment of Catholics (and those of other denominations as well) have come to feel at ease identifying themselves religiously as "Christian" when earlier their religious identity focused on being "Catholic." Even some who have drifted away from overt connection with the institutional Catholic Church have kept a belief in and a devotion to Christ.

It is perfectly logical that returning Jesus to the center of Christians' religious awareness should deeply influence their participation in eucharist. As we will see in the next chapter, our clearer understanding of Jesus' resurrection means the eucharist is increasingly viewed as an encounter with the risen Christ. But who exactly is this risen Jesus whom we so encounter? While his present state of risen life certainly involves some basic change, this risen Christ is still the same person, Jesus of Nazareth, with the same mission. So knowing more accurately what his life and activity were during the few short decades of his earthly career lets us know more accurately who the Jesus is that Christians encounter in eucharist as the Christ. Obviously, what a group of Christians believe about Jesus of Nazareth is bound to condition their encounter with him in the liturgy.

Moreover, as we said, the eucharistic action is of its essence a remembrance of Jesus, especially of his dying and rising. God's saving action in Jesus is what the ritual recalls and celebrates. From the very beginning the element of "remembering" was associated with the emerging eucharistic celebration. The words of institution recorded in the gospels and in Paul's letter to the Corinthians declare "This is my body; this is my blood" but then add: "Do this in *memory* of me." Over the centuries, this explicit statement of remembrance has remained essential to the eucharistic prayer. It is clear, then, how important it is for Christians approaching the eucharistic action to know who was and is this Jesus they are remembering.

One of the recent developments in Catholic faith that is linked with the recovery of Jesus' humanity is the acceptance and appreciation of religious experience. Given the prominence in recent decades of things like the Cursillo or the charismatic movement, we tend to forget that until the mid-twentieth century religious experience was suspect in official Catholic circles. "Religious experience" smacked of a person's *emotions* and was therefore considered too subjective and untrustworthy. Faith, on the other hand, was explained as a *rational* assent to the evidence that Catholic doctrine was true. Then, for a number of reasons, we came to accept and even emphasize one's personal relationship to God and to see faith as essentially such a relationship. If eucharist itself is the epitome of this experiential approach to faith, an encounter with the risen Christ and through him to God, it is apparent how fundamental to eucharistic participation is the understanding people have of this risen Jesus they encounter.

The Eucharist and the Church

However there is still another element of critical study that relates to Jesus and the eucharist. What did Jesus himself do to "institute the eucharist"? Popular understanding has tended to view the Last Supper as "the first Mass" and even see it as the occasion when Jesus ordained his disciples as "the first priests." Neither of these is accurate. Jesus did not himself establish any of the ritual forms of Christianity, nor did he ordain anyone. Historical research into the origins of Christianity makes it rather clear that ritual forms like the eucharist only gradually came into being in the first few decades of the church. Like the New Testament scriptures, the criterion of authenticity for Christian liturgies was *apostolic* origin—the creed we still recite lists as the notes of the church "one, holy, catholic and *apostolic*."

The fact that the ritual form of eucharist was not established by Jesus himself gives the church of today much greater flexibility in creating ritual patterns that fit the faith and lives of people in different cultural contexts. The liturgy is the church's creation. Granted that this happens with the inspiration and guidance of Christ's Spirit, so it isn't a purely human activity, yet what Christians once did they can still do: Find appropriate ways to remember and make truly present the mystery of Jesus' dying and rising.

The question "What did Jesus himself do to accomplish his mission of bringing about the reign of God?" extends beyond the question of his institution of the eucharist. It challenges the way Christians today share in eucharistic ritual. Eucharist continues Jesus' proclamation of the arrival of God's reign, and like Jesus' original proclamation it demands continuing conversion. To take but one element of Jesus' public ministry: Careful reading of the gospels makes it quite clear that Jesus taught and lived out a preferential option for the poor. Present-day Christian evangelization, expressed most fully in the eucharist, cannot avoid proclaiming this same social attitude. The "Amen" at the end of the eucharistic prayer and even more so the reception of communion cannot be genuine and at the same time reject acceptance of this special care for the poor.

Catholics as they share in eucharist are not at liberty to dream up a Jesus for themselves, a Jesus who leaves them comfortable and complacent in a world that sadly needs the healing which is central to Christian discipleship. Eucharist is meant to be Christianity's central profession of faith, a faith that continues to be a counter-cultural view of life because Jesus himself taught and lived a counter-cultural gospel. His way of healing contradicted the power brokers of his day—and, for that matter, of our day. An actual celebration of eucharist will be very different depending upon whether the assembled Catholics agree with this gospel or not.

The experience of eucharist is meant to be a personal encounter with Christ who is present in this moment. It is more than an encounter with Jesus of Nazareth through memory, the kind that one has while reading the biography of a great figure from the past. In the eucharist we encounter a person who is *now*, because Jesus is risen. So our insight into earliest Christianity's understanding of Jesus' resurrection is one of the more important roots of today's liturgical change.

4

The Risen Christ

It is seldom that a theological breakthrough can be precisely dated, but such was the case with the publication of Francis Durrwell's book, *The Resurrection*, in mid-century. Actually the insights contained in that volume emerged from a decades-long period of careful textual study and reflection, especially at the Biblical Institute in Rome and the Ecole Biblique in Jerusalem, but with the appearance of Durrwell's book it became apparent that a major advance had been made in understanding the nature of Jesus' "rising from the dead."

Like so much of recent theological insight we think of as "new," the understanding of Jesus' passage into risen life that emerged in recent decades is not an innovation but a recovery of very early Christian understandings that did not receive full formulation in their day or were obscured by later developments.

The Risen Christ Is with Us

Examination of the New Testament passages dealing with Jesus' after-death existence as the Christ has helped us realize how earth-shaking the experience of the Risen One was for the disciples. Nothing like it had happened before; no word or category of thought adequately expressed it. The closest thing was the notion—still vague in Jewish understanding—of the "rising from the dead" which presumably would happen to the just on "the day of the Lord." So, even though it was something different and unexpected, the word "resurrection" was applied to Jesus' passage into risen life. After all, this was clearly "the day of the Lord."

Attempts to explain this happening to themselves and to converts to this new revelation took a story form—actually several story forms in the traditions that eventually were preserved in the gospels and Pauline writings. Underneath these narratives, quite clearly catechetical in nature, one can discern certain common elements of belief: The Jesus they had known and saw die was not dead but alive; he was not a ghost but this same person, truly alive; he was not someone else but the same Jesus, and he still related to them in friendship; but he enjoyed a new state of human existence, having triumphed over death.

Central to the apostles' experience was the awareness that Jesus was still present to them. This awareness finds expression in the final words of Matthew's gospel: "Behold I am with you always, even to the end of the world." Even in the gospel of Luke, which for theological reasons pictures Jesus' passage into a superior way of human life as a "going up," the scene of the two disciples on the way to Emmaus expresses the conviction of early Christians that the risen Christ was with them, especially in "the breaking of the bread." Over the centuries, however, this sense of Christ's constant presence to believers gave way to the notion that Jesus had left this earth and gone up to heaven. It is only in mid-twentieth century that we have regained a more accurate understanding that the risen Lord is always present to the community of believers.

One could go on at length about the nature of Christ's risen existence, about its implications for the whole of Christian faith and life, but our interest here is to highlight the way this belief affected the celebration of eucharist. Actually, it has deeply affected both theological reflection on eucharist and the actual participation of people in this ritual. Without going into any detail, the theology about the eucharist has been moved into an entirely new dimension where classical notions like the eucharist as sacrifice, the eucharistic presence, transubstantiation, and the eucharistic causation of "grace" are undergoing, not denial, but a radical rethinking. On the level of eucharistic celebration, which concerns us here, it has initiated a basic shift in what Catholics believe about Jesus' presence and about what occurs, or at least ought to occur, in the eucharistic action.

To appreciate the change that is happening, it may be helpful to recall the understanding of resurrection that prevailed until very recently. Imagine a country church where Mass was celebrated once on Sunday by a pastor from the neighboring town and where, because of the little church's isolation, there was no reservation of the Blessed Sacrament during the week. When people gathered for Mass, standing outside and sharing neighborhood news as they waited for Father to arrive, they had no awareness of Jesus being there yet. The presence of Jesus would have to wait for Mass, more specifically for the consecration of the bread and wine, at which point he would be with them for a short time. Christ became present, in a way the people considered more or less miraculous, with the words of consecration. He would become more intimately present to each of them with communion. Then, with the end of Mass, he would be gone again for another week.

In the neighboring town where the consecrated hosts were kept in the tabernacle during the week, the perception of what occurred at Mass would be the same, except that the reservation of the Blessed Sacrament meant Jesus remained with them in the tabernacle. These Catholics had the opportunity, which country folk did not, of visiting the church when they wished and there being again in the presence of Christ. However, outside the church building itself, Christ was not wherever they were.

While we're now aware that understanding was inadequate, its central belief was true and precious: The risen Christ was, at least at times, still with us, was interested in us, and was our savior and friend. The view was inadequate insofar as it *limited* Christ's presence to certain times and places and with a specific geographical place. Realizing the true character of Christ's resurrection has extended our understanding of Christ's presence, gradually making us aware—as Pope Paul VI taught in his encyclical on the eucharist—that the fundamental presence of the risen Christ is in the people of faith. Even the presence we experience in the eucharistic consecration of bread and wine is presence to the assembled people in proportion to their faith.

Several other understandings were linked with this. Because the risen Christ has not gone away to some distant heaven but remains with believers, these believers really function as "the Body of Christ." It is not incidental that the recovered awareness of the church as "Body of Christ" has come about at the same time as our deepened insight into "resurrection."

The Community Celebrates

Again, since mid-century we have gradually come to see that the principal celebrant of any eucharist is the risen Christ himself. It is his self-gift to the gathered Christians that sacramentalizes and proclaims the glory of God. This can occur because those assembled people are the Body of Christ. By implication, the visible celebrant of any eucharist is the community that is there, which obviously has required us to reinterpret the distinctive role of the ordained presider in the celebrating community.

What this means—and the meaning is only beginning to be appreciated—is that the very character of *people's participation* in eucharist is quite different than we thought. We knew after Vatican II's *Constitution on the Sacred Liturgy*, if not before, that those at Mass were meant to be actively involved in what was happening, but the nature of that participation wasn't clear. We knew people should understand what was going on so, at least in their own inner awareness, they could join their belief and commitment to that of the ordained presider. But we are only slowly realizing that the participation of the community means more than that: It means that the entire community *does* the eucharistic action, though individuals may have specialized roles within that community action. The liturgical leader presides, but it is the community that celebrates.

Slow Shift in Attitudes

When Catholics assemble for the eucharistic action, what do they expect to happen? What do they think they, themselves, are doing? It would be naive to suggest that the shift in understanding described above has yet affected a basic change in most Catholics. At the same time, the eucharistic experience of people has begun to reflect this shift. Laity are being assigned roles in the proclamation of biblical texts and in the distribution of communion. The fact that the ordained leader is increasingly referred to as "the presider" rather than "the celebrant" means that people are beginning to experience the eucharist as the community's action. In the small intentional communities springing up across the world this sense of "doing" the eucharist is even more prominent.

Depending on the speed that current theological clarifications filter down to popular understanding, the experience of eucharistic celebration will continue to be altered. It is the shift in the understandings that people bring to eucharist that constitutes the fundamental change taking place. In time it will almost certainly begin to make the externals of the eucharist more appropriately expressive of the faith of the gathered communities.

This need not imply that radical alteration of the liturgical ritual will occur or needs to occur. Ritual, as the principal conveyor of tradition, is by nature conservative in the deepest sense of that term. What does have to happen, and is already beginning to happen, is that the eucharist functions more authentically *as a ritual.* Rituals are actions in which groups of people say together who they are as individuals and as a community. In these actions people come to discover more deeply their history and their identity and pass on this discovery to a younger generation. By these actions they accept responsibility as individuals and as a community to preserve and develop the community and to work together to achieve its purpose for existing. Because the identity and purpose of the church are intimately linked with the risen Christ, the "new" awareness of the risen Christ present to the community of believers promises to make the eucharistic ritual a more genuine celebration of Christian belief and mission.

Perhaps the impact on people's understanding of what they should be doing at the eucharist can be succinctly explained by answering the question: What does the risen Christ say to the Christian assembly through the ritual of the Mass? Eucharist is a liturgy of the word; but the "word" in question is primarily Christ himself, whom God still speaks to humans as God's own Word. But what does the risen Christ say to the eucharistic community? The same thing that he said to his disciples at the Last Supper.

If one reads the accounts of the Supper, especially in John's gospel, it is clear that Jesus related to his friends on that occasion in deep friendship. Whether through the act of foot washing or through the giving of bread and wine as his body and blood, what he was saying to his own was "Here I am for you as your friend, so that you may have life and joy. I am here to serve you by the gift of myself." This word has continued in his risen existence as the narratives of the Easter and post-Easter "apparitions" attest.

This is still said in the eucharist. The ritual symbolism of eucharist proclaims Jesus' self-gift to the gathered Christians, and it challenges them to respond in kind. Eucharist can be a source of individual and community transformation only when Christ is *risen* and *now* and *present*. Eucharistic liturgy should lead a community to deepening its awareness of the presence of the risen Christ. As this happens, the experience of eucharist, its concrete reality, will inevitably become something quite other than "attending Mass."

5

An Evolving Church

The enhanced understanding of Christ's resurrection is certainly central to the outlook which U.S. Catholics bring to the eucharist. Yet it is only one of several elements in the changing perception of themselves as "church." Our understanding of sacraments has been affected in the past half century by a growing awareness, in both theological and popular circles, of their ecclesial dimension, their close relationship to the church. It isn't always clear *how* the whole church is involved in the ritual actions that occur throughout the world, but there is an increasing sense that a sacramental action is more than a religious pipeline through which "grace" flows from God to a person through an ordained celebrant. Somehow the church plays a role.

People's understanding of the church's role in sacramental liturgies like the eucharist is vague and anything but homogeneous, for the simple reason that there are widely differing views about what "church" means. There is a great deal of discussion today about the ideological diversity within U.S. Catholics. Our church includes people of conservative bent who are—or at least are accused of being—reluctant to move in the progressive paths suggested by Vatican II and those who are more eager for fundamental change of the church. As a result, different people have quite different views of the way the eucharist plays a role in the life of the church. Still, beneath these differences there are certain shared views that in varying degrees mark most Catholics' image of "church" and therefore of the eucharist as an action of the church. Perhaps the best way of getting at the underlying understandings of "church" is to ask the question: What does it mean for people to identify themselves as "Catholic"?

What Is Distinctly Catholic?

Many students of U.S. society considered the election of John F. Kennedy as a sign that Catholicism had joined the mainstream of U.S. life. There seems little doubt that since then Catholics have become increasingly prominent and accepted in public life; they are no longer "the others." As a result Catholics no longer think of themselves as outsiders among the Protestant majority. To some extent this has raised the question, "Then what does it mean to be Catholic?" Although the response to the question has been varied, the element of defensiveness vis-à-vis U.S. culture has largely disappeared. Catholics come to eucharist quite satisfied with being "American" and no longer see their parish as a refuge from cultural alienation or Sunday Mass attendance as fidelity to being non-Protestant.

Catholic identity has become less of a denominational thing. As a matter of fact, U.S. Catholics have become far more ecumenical in outlook. They are more likely today to regard members of other churches as fellow Christians. This hasn't diminished their belief in the eucharist or its distinctiveness among religious services carried on in Christian churches. There is, though, a subtle assumption that the worship of other groups, especially rituals like the Lutheran "Lord's Supper" or the Episcopalian "Holy Communion," is equally Christian and "eucharistic." Catholics come to Mass on Sunday with lessened feeling of being "the only true Church." Though they probably wouldn't express it that way, many Catholics have come to think of themselves and of what they do as "being Christian" rather than simply "belonging to the Catholic Church."

There can be a negative aspect to the increased identity of Catholics as being "American." It may indicate they have been coopted by the consumer society. On the other hand it may bring with it a new sense of responsibility for making U.S. society what it could and should be. Eucharist as covenant pledge to work for the establishment of God's reign can—precisely because of this sense of "being American"—lead U.S. Catholics to minister to their country. It is hard to imagine such an outlook among first-generation immigrants who celebrated the eucharist as an assertion of their ethnic culture.

The People Are the Church

Probably more important in its impact on eucharistic celebration is the acceptance, shared to some extent by all the differing groups in the U.S. Catholic Church, of Vatican II's teaching that the entire people of God constitutes the church. The previously-accepted identification of "the church" with official leadership has not vanished; in many circles it is still very much alive. However, there has been across the board a sense of ownership that was rare, if it existed at all, three generations ago. Both traditionalists and progressives are as vocal as they are, as committed as they are to their positions, precisely because they consider it *their* church. This has resulted in a greater seriousness about the eucharistic ritual than was the case before the council.

Owning this new sense of "being church," many Catholics today take it for granted that they should be active in the liturgy. This has been reinforced by the postconciliar openness to lay women and men exercising roles as lectors, eucharistic ministers and acolytes and by the training and employment of lay people as parish directors of liturgy. Even the geography of sacred space, with the altar closer to and facing the people, has conveyed the understanding that the eucharist is the action of the entire assembly, not only of the ordained presider. Many Catholics today come to Mass with the expectation of doing something, not simply the expectation of something being done for them. The shift in their theology of the church has clearly led to a shift in their theology of the eucharist.

Social Pressures and Church Attendance

Another subtle but important shift has been in the gradual elimination of ethnic parishes. In small towns as well as in large cities the older pattern was that of Catholic churches being "the Irish church," "the Polish church" or "the German church," depending on which immigrant groups lived in that particular neighborhood. As these immigrant groups became assimilated and became "American," the identification of parishes along ethnic lines has lessened, and in many cases has completely disappeared. This resulted in changing attitudes toward attendance at Sunday Mass. Mass was no longer something that continued the patterns of inherited culture—a family tradition which children were expected to follow. Social pressures about committing mortal sin once induced Catholics to be faithful to their eucharistic responsibilities. For many young Catholics today such motivations are not effective. As a result, they have abandoned regular involvement with the eucharist.

This mindset that viewed eucharistic practice as a way of carrying on ethnic traditions was a symptom of a larger change in attitude: Being Catholic was a central element in the identity of many families. Religious traditions, including regular attendance at Sunday Mass, were a basic exercise of identity. Children grew up knowing that Sunday morning meant going to church with their parents. For many of them Sunday eucharist was not religiously or personally meaningful, but they continued attending for family reasons. Even after leaving home for college a large number still came to Sunday Mass—not because it really represented a time of closer relationship to God (which, fortunately, it not infrequently does) but because that was what they are supposed to do on Sunday.

These attitudes have been changing. Participating in the eucharist, especially in the Sunday liturgy, for most Catholics has become more a deliberate choice rather than a family habit. People are not content simply to be at Mass. They are looking for liturgical situations that show signs of life, that offer the opportunity for awakening and expression of their faith. People who a few years ago would always have gone on Sunday to their neighborhood parish are now "shopping around." On Catholic college campuses the late night, less formal liturgies celebrated in dormitories often attract standing-room-only crowds of students who come because they want to be there. Unfortunately, many other people have just drifted away from eucharistic practice that ceased to have any meaning for them.

Beneath this observable phenomenon lies a "new" assumption of what it means to be a Catholic. There is growing awareness of the church as *community*. People, young and old, gratefully experience such community when it exists. They miss it and seek it when it does not exist. Somehow, too, they have an instinctive realization that eucharist is central to Catholic community. It can be a cause of community but cannot be what it should be unless it celebrates to some degree a community already in existence.

Very few Catholics have a formulated theology about the church. What more and more of them are acquiring is a grassroots-level understanding of Christianity that is both more accurate and more faith-filled. Such a "folk theology," if it is nurtured, will be the source of a liturgical revolution in the deepest sense of that term.

Without being naively optimistic, one can see signs that the revolution is already under way. In many parishes around the country—for that matter around the world—the teaching of Vatican II that Christianity should be marked by genuine sharing of faith is being translated into a new sense of community. As Catholics develop a different experience of parish or other forms of community, they inevitably think differently about themselves as Catholics, as the church. And just as inevitably, they do not come to eucharist as a gathering of many individuals in the same space at the same time to observe an ordained person preside at a sacred action on their behalf. They come as a community of believers. They come to eucharist *together* to do something together because they are the people of God.

6

Celebrating Christian Life

W hen the liturgical revival began in the early part of this century, it was repeatedly asked how the celebration of the Mass has more of an effect on people's lives. That same concern was clearly voiced in Vatican II's document on the liturgy which insisted that people understand what was going on at Mass in order for it to have a salutary effect on their Christian faith and life.

What was not voiced, except very implicitly, was the effect that people's lives had on the liturgical ritual itself. At that time the notion was still prevalent that the ordained presider was the one who did the action and that the assembled congregation merely attended Mass. There was no notion of input from the people; theirs was a receptive role. This view extended beyond the eucharist to other Christian rituals. The language used reflected that view that people "*received* the sacraments."

After all, if the eucharistic ritual acted automatically (which was the way that most understood the phrase *ex opere operato*), the only essentials were that the presider be ordained, follow exactly the words and actions of the liturgy, and have the intention of doing what the church intended.

For centuries people had debated the influence that the faith and holiness of this presider might have on the effectiveness of sacraments; there had even been a formal condemnation of the heresy of Donatism which maintained that an ordained minister could not validly effect a sacrament while in the state of grave sin. But few people considered whether the state of soul of the assembled Christians might change the "objective" reality of the eucharistic ritual, although they acknowledged it might condition the extent to which people received grace from that ritual.

The Sacramentality of Experience

What we now know theoretically and are beginning to realize practically is that the interaction between the eucharist and people's Christian lives is a two-way street. Eucharist is not simply a formalized ritual action performed as a public celebration; it is a group of Christians' *experience* of the meaning of their lives, and *as such* it influences those lives. While a certain recognizable similarity among rituals is needed to maintain the unity of Christian faith, the concrete reality is that no two celebrations of eucharist can be exactly the same, because the celebrating communities are always in some respects different.

What happens in the eucharist is that the meaning of people's Christian lives interprets the gospel message that is proclaimed, and that gospel message, in turn, throws new light on the meaning of their lives. The gospel message proclaimed in the eucharistic action is meant to transform people's understanding of what it means to be human, so a given group's daily experience of being human in their actual life situation will inevitably affect how they hear that word. At the heart of the eucharistic proclamation is the mystery of death transformed by resurrection; what a group of people actually hear depends on the view of death and life they already possess. The gospel proclaimed is always a call to further conversion, but each individual or group will hear that call filtered through their present attitudes, goals and values. Inevitably, the human reality of the community gathered for eucharist will condition the experienced reality of that eucharist. Because that experienced reality is what it is, it will have a specific effect on the people individually and on their shared life as a Christian community.

All this would seem to be just common sense, if—as is the case—the eucharist is an action of the entire community rather than the action of the presider alone. However, there is a deeper dimension that can only be known in faith. Beyond the fact that people's social location, economic situation, ethnic/racial background, educational level and status in society influence the way they interpret things that happen to them, lies the *sacramentality* of their experience. Discovering and accepting this sacramentality is one of the most important "new" elements in Catholics' faith today and therefore in their involvement in eucharist.

Very briefly, because God is present and active in people's lives, those lives are a "word" about this God. Actually, for each of us, our own experience of ourselves as we go through the days and years of our life is the primary word that tells us about God in relation to us. I may be well acquainted with the scriptures and their message about God in relation to humans, I may be well educated about traditional Christian teaching about God, but what more than anything else tells me about God in relation to me is my experience of being me. That basic word is often ambiguous and needs interpretation. It has depths that only faith, guided by scripture and Christian teaching, can discover. Yet in that deeper discovery we come to believe the unbelievable: *God is for us in profound friendship.*

As we become more aware and open up to the gift of God's self, the divine presence transforms the entirety of our life. What this means is that the "ordinary" elements of our experience carry God-meaning, something that runs counter to the prevalent belief that God intervenes only in extraordinary events. Of course there can be exceptional moments in our lives when we are blessed with a keener awareness of God's being for us; special conversion experiences do happen, and when they do they constitute a great blessing. However we are more aware today that God is present in the "ordinary," in our successes and sufferings, in our growing up and aging, in our loving and being loved, in our dealings with one another. Because God is so present, our lives in their entirety—most specially in those ordinary things that are part and parcel of every human's life—take on a new depth of meaning. This is another way of saying that our lives are *sacramental* to the degree that we become aware of this involvement of the divine with us. It is this sacramentality that we celebrate when we gather in gratitude for the eucharist.

The Grace of God's Presence

One of the insights that has helped us appreciate the ordinary course of our lives is recent reflection on the human career of Jesus himself. Without abandoning the central Christian belief in Jesus' unique relationship as Son to his heavenly Abba, we have been weaned from some of the semi-miraculous characteristics we had previously attributed to Jesus. We now accept that he truly was human as are we, that he grew up and discovered his identity through daily experiences as we do, that he had to learn, that he made mistakes and was limited in his knowledge by living in one culture at one point in history. But because of the unique presence to him of God as his Abba and his unique openness to that presence, the regular fabric of human experience took on a depth of meaning it had never had before. Even the meaning of death was reversed. Out of Jesus' dying as a witness to truth and love there emerged the unending life that is our destiny as human persons. This is the very heart of Jesus' transformation of human life, the very heart of his saving role in human history, the heart of the gospel that is still proclaimed when Christians gather for eucharist. No human life is "ordinary," because God is part of each life.

In eucharistic ritual, the Jesus-meaning and the meaning of the assembled believers encounter and interpret one another. One could use technical language and say that the hermeneutic with which people approach eucharist conditions the reality of eucharist. In simpler language, those who come to eucharist hear the message of the words and actions in the ritual in the light of their own understanding of what their human and Christian lives are all about; and on the other hand the message proclaimed in the ritual gives them a new perspective on the meaning of their lives. This gospel message transforms the significance of their daily experience and consequently transforms them. It gives grace.

Most Catholics have not understood "grace" this way. If they thought about "grace" at all, it probably suggested special helps that God gives in times of decision or "temptation." Or it had to do with "being in the state of grace"—basically in a good relationship with God and free from any grave sin. Grace had been thought of as *something,* but its exact character was not clear. However sanctifying grace is not some *thing;* instead it is the transformation of a person that results from the presence of God to that person. This presence of God to humans is not a reality that comes and goes, as if God relates actively to us only at times. Instead, the divine offer of friendship is constant and depends only on that human acceptance which is faith.

Because God's presence is meant to transfuse and transform the entirety of our human lives, even the most ordinary elements of our lives are sacramental in the full sense. They possess a new depth of meaning because of God's being for us. And because the actuality of our human lives is the sequence of experiences in which we discover and establish our individual identity, changing the meaning of those experiences changes us as persons. As people become more aware of the sacramentality of life, they can bring the awareness to eucharist and make the eucharist what it is meant to be: A community celebrating the fact that this is what our lives are all about.

The more that Catholics experience the eucharist this way as an encounter with a loving God who is revealed in the loving self-gift of the risen Christ, the less do they come to Mass with a sense of their sinfulness and alienation from God. Certainly the need for admission of human frailty and sin endures, and the eucharistic liturgy needs to express this. But the confession of sin ought to take second place to rejoicing at the wonder of the new life offered to us. Recognition of our sinful alienation from one another and from God no longer carries an overbearing sense of guilt and becomes instead a realistic assessment of our constant need for reconciliation. This represents a basic shift in the experienced reality of eucharist that has already begun to find expression in liturgical ceremonies such as the giving of peace.

The intersection of Christians' lives with their celebration of eucharist points to the need for a fearless and creative approach to the issue of inculturation. Granted, the adaptation of eucharistic liturgy to the various human cultures in which Christians live is a delicate task, for it is critically important that diversity of liturgical language and gesture doesn't lose the central symbolisms of Christian worship. However, unless the symbolisms intrinsic to eucharist, symbolisms that link us with the historical reality of Jesus and with his continuing presence among us, interact with the symbolisms that control our culture and lives, the eucharist will not touch us deeply or transform us individually and as communities.

Above all, it is in the shared symbols that are truly active in our culture that we find the deeper meaning of our existence. Theoretical analyses can clarify what's occurring in our lives, but only in the symbolic language of music and art and poetry and dance do imagination and passion become awakened, intuitions occur and action result. Any good preacher knows that the imaginative use of metaphor and picture-language can lead to conversion, while purely rational explanations often leave hearers untouched. However for such conversion to spring from eucharist—as it should—the poetry, imagery, metaphors and music must be the kind that already resonates with people in their distinctive culture.

Eucharist celebrates the wonder of human life experienced as the mystery of God's saving love manifested in Jesus' dying and rising. For that to happen, Christians must learn that this is what eucharist is all about.

7

The Power of
Eucharistic Ritual

We ended the last chapter describing "grace" as the transformation of a person that takes place because of the presence of God to that person. Most Catholics, of course, because they are unaccustomed to technical theological discussion, wouldn't describe grace exactly that way. However, there is a growing understanding about the way the eucharist transforms us. It doesn't occur in some semimagical manner. Instead, it is the way people share what is happening in eucharist that makes a difference in its impact on them. Participation in the eucharist ought to change people. They know it; increasingly they appreciate that change doesn't come from *routine* Sunday observance.

Liturgical developments since Vatican II have certainly reinforced this view. The revised liturgy for the baptism of adults (the RCIA) drew attention again to an individual's choice of real personal faith and conversion. Eucharistic celebrations animated by the principles of the council's decree on the liturgy attempt to deepen our relationship to the God revealed in Jesus instead of drawing on the merits of Jesus' death to atone for human sinfulness. But if celebrating the eucharist is meant to change people for the better, make them more thoroughly Christian, how does it do it?

The Way Rituals Work

The question isn't just theoretical. Unless we're clear about what the eucharist is meant to achieve and the means it uses, how can we plan creative and effective liturgical celebrations? People do have some notion of the goal: The celebration makes the risen Christ increasingly present to and influential in people's lives, gradually forges the assembled Christians into a true community of believers, brings the assembled Christians to a realistic acceptance of Christianity's mission of justice and peace in the world. Still, many people would be hard pressed to tell you exactly how the eucharist works to further these goals.

The simple answer to this—an answer we will unpack in the rest of this chapter—is that the eucharist works in the way *rituals* work, because the eucharist is in essence a ritual. Fortunately recent years have seen a good deal of study on ritual and its role in human societies. There has been considerable study of Christian liturgical rituals. We can draw on those studies to describe quickly how the eucharist's effectiveness as a ritual is one of the principal changes taking place today. To keep our discussion from becoming too theoretical, it may help to compare the eucharistic ritual to some of the family rituals we take for granted.

When families gather for special occasions such as Christmas (gatherings that almost always involve a festive meal) they become more conscious of their family identity.

It's not that they forget their membership in this particular family during the regular course of their lives. But many things occupy their consciousness then—their work, personal cares, involvement with friends and simply coping with the problems of everyday life—with the result that they don't focus on their larger family. However, when they do get together for Christmas they automatically recall their *identity* as members of one extended family.

Similarly, the members of a given parish are fully occupied during the week with business affairs, taking care of their homes and one another, socializing with their friends, etc. They know they are Catholics, but that fact is not usually in the forefront of their consciousness. When, however, they gather on Sunday for the eucharist, whether anyone draws attention to it or not, they think of themselves as Catholics. As a matter of fact, for many of them, coming to Mass on Sunday is exactly what it means for them to be Catholic. Ideally, then, when they celebrate eucharist together the nature of their *Christian identity* is challenged and deepened by the liturgy, so that gradually they understand better and personally accept more fully the implications of the gospel they hear proclaimed. This change doesn't happen in a hidden or mysterious way because "grace" is being given to them. It happens through the effectiveness of the liturgy itself—whether or not it clearly communicates the good news that the risen Christ is present, and whether or not those gathered are open to that communication.

Just as with a family, persons gathered for eucharist are not meant to deepen only their individual awareness of family identity. The eucharistic gathering ought to increase people's understanding that they are a *community of faith* in Christ and deepen their commitment to be such a community. This is probably one of the most noticeable shifts in people's eucharistic celebration in recent years. There is new awareness of and interest in being a community of believing Christians, and celebrating the eucharist together is the core action of their shared Christian life. One needs to avoid exaggeration in describing this shift: It is not universal, and in many cases it is only incipient, but it is hard to deny that "community" has become more prominent in Christian self-awareness.

How Ritual Shapes Community

Rituals not only tell a group that they are a community; they describe in symbolic ways the nature of the sharing that makes them a community. Often when one joins some club or organization there is an initiation ritual with distinctive symbolic actions that say something about the kind of club involved. Children in school learn that they are citizens of this country by the daily practice of the pledge of allegiance. Poring over photo albums when families gather for the holidays is an important sharing that symbolizes their identity with one another as this particular family.

Similarly, in the eucharistic action, the assembled Christians experience themselves as a community of believers in and disciples of the risen Christ. One aspect of this that is changing for many Catholics, particularly young people, is the awareness people have of being Christians gathered together rather than people who go to a Catholic church on Sunday rather than to a Lutheran or Methodist service. This is partly due to the fact that Catholics are more exposed today to the eucharistic celebrations of other mainline Christian churches. The similarity of the rituals being celebrated creates a sense of solidarity with other believing Christians.

Another aspect of rituals' effect on a group of people has only recently been explicitly recognized and has quickly become a neuralgic issue of discussion. In subtle but real ways rituals reflect and reinforce the lines of power and authority in a group. The fact that a family always gathers for Thanksgiving at the grandparents' home and that the grandparents always decide exactly how the dinner will proceed points to the esteem and personal power the grandparents have in the extended family.

When it comes to the eucharist, the liturgical role of the ordained presider is the most powerful source of his authority and power in the congregation. True, the official empowerment of that man came through sacramental ordination, but in the actual life of the community his role in the eucharistic ritual, a role understood as mediator between the assembled people and God, gives him uncontested sacred power. As we noted, however, the recent theology of eucharist makes it clearer that the entire community acts as celebrant of the liturgy. The presider exercises his distinctive role as a member of the community rather than a person who stands between the community and God. At the same time many women became conscious of the extent to which the exclusion of women from full liturgical ministry was rooted in social structures of male domination. Indeed, their exclusion helped perpetuate those structures.

We now understand that some liturgical forms, particularly the language used, must be altered if the eucharistic assembly is to symbolize the full equality that is meant to mark a Christian community. As the symbolic message of the eucharist evolves so that it no longer confirms male superiority, the shift in power already taking place in the church will be intensified. Not only is the eucharistic liturgy changing, the church is changing. The eucharist is both a reflection and an agent of that change.

A Covenant People

In all likelihood the changes occurring in the externals of the liturgy are irreversible. Change will continue, but the pace of change will depend upon people's awareness of what they are doing and their willingness to go along with the implications of eucharistic symbolism. Eucharist is the central image in the life of the church of the covenant between God and humans that began at least as far back as Moses. Gospel descriptions of Jesus' mission portray it as the fulfillment of the Mosaic/Davidic covenant, and this portrayal finds its culminating expression in the words spoken by Jesus at the Supper: "This is the cup of the new covenant in my blood."

Accepting this covenant enacted in eucharist, a covenant focused on the risen Christ present to the community as the living pledge that unites humans and God, means that those sharing eucharist share also in that pledge. Like the ancient baptismal formula that forbade discrimination in the church between rich or poor, slave or free, Jew or Gentile, male or female, today's eucharist calls Catholics to honor and implement the absolute equality of all persons by working to abolish discriminations. Like the covenant of Israel that fixed just relations among humans as the measure of their relation to God, the eucharistic community itself is meant by its pursuit of justice to be a sacrament of humanity's relationship to God.

Such a requirement is unavoidable if one is serious about the character of the eucharistic liturgy. Christians are increasingly aware of it. From the very beginning of the modern liturgical revival, even before Vatican II, there was a clear link between authentic eucharistic celebration and the commitment to social justice. It isn't accidental that Vatican II itself, whose first major act was the document on the liturgy, then went on to the *Constitution on the Church in the Modern World* which represented a dramatic shift in the church toward involvement in social change. It would be naive to expect that all Catholics have responded to this challenge and moved toward equality and justice for all, but the fact that people increasingly know the challenge exists represents a fundamental change in the approach to the eucharist.

Clearly, a deeper vision of Christianity and its celebration of eucharist is coming to fore in the church today. So is the incentive that urges those who share eucharist to accept its challenge to responsible discipleship. Since a ritual acts neither by itself, nor as magic, nor automatically, the ritual effectiveness of the eucharist is itself the principal agent in obtaining those two objectives—*provided eucharist functions as a true symbol, a genuine ritual.* So what can we do to have this happen?

8

What To Do?

We have noted that the shifts taking place in the celebration of the eucharist are deeper than the observable changes in liturgy or the changes in frequency caused by declining numbers of ordained persons. These deeper shifts have to do with understandings and attitudes people today are bringing—or not bringing—to the celebration. If this is true, what are we to do about it?

First of all, there is no reason for panic because of the increasing shortage of ordained men, though there certainly is room for honest concern. While regularity of eucharistic practice is a basic element in maturing Christian faith, there is nothing consecrated about the *exact frequency* with which a given community celebrates eucharist. What's much more important is the openness and intensity and awareness with which the liturgy is celebrated. Not that one would advocate dropping Mass each Sunday, but eucharist celebrated once a month with careful preparation leading up to it, with the assembled congregation aware of what is happening, actively involved and committed to following out the proclaimed gospel, would create more of a eucharistic community than

perfunctory liturgies each Sunday of the month. The ideal,
of course, is to have careful celebrations each Sunday

In the early days of the Catholic Church in the United
States, it was not uncommon for an immigrant group on the
edges of the expanding country to be without eucharist for
weeks on end. When the traveling priest was not available,
the people would gather for prayer, most often in their own
homes, instruct their children in the faith and continue religious practices that were part of their culture back in the
home country. For the most part Christian faith not only sur-
vived but flourished in these situations. When eucharist was
celebrated it probably had more effect because it was special
and cherished. No one wants to go back to those earlier
times, because the greater availability of eucharist has been a
key element in the emergence of a vital Catholic community
in this country. However, the memory of that earlier time
does provide some assurance that the present prospect of
fewer celebrations of eucharist can be met positively.

Eucharist and Everyday Life

What, then, can be done to profit by our deeper understanding and the other deep-down changes we have mentioned so that the positive movement toward a better liturgy
can be sustained and reinforced? Certainly, we need to celebrate eucharistic liturgies that create a *sense of awe* because of
the presence of God, a presence that is grounded in an unbelievable intimacy of the divine with us humans. This is more
possible now because we better understand what the resurrection of Jesus is all about. To know that the eucharistic
presence of the risen Christ is primarily his offer of friendship and not simply with the changing of bread and wine—

though that change is intrinsic to his offer—can lead a group gathered for eucharist to realize and wonder at the "condescension" of God's offer of intimacy with them. This is the real mystery of the eucharist. It is not something hidden and secret but revealed in all its unbelievableness.

Obviously, such awesome eucharistic celebration requires *understanding* on the part of the assembly that this divine offer is taking place. The assembly needs to be told that the ordained presider is not the primary agent of the liturgy, told that he is not a replacement, a stand-in, for Christ because he acts "in persona Christi." Instead the people need to know that the primary agent of any eucharist is Christ himself; the eucharist is his action of giving self to those who believe in him. This action of Christ can take place precisely because the assembled community (including the presider who has a distinctive role) is "body of Christ." The awe this creates is not something extraordinary and "out of this world." It is always awesome to be loved unconditionally by another person, and it is intensified when the lover is the risen Christ who sacramentalizes the God he knows as lover.

Eucharistic liturgies of this kind need to *emerge from the life* of the celebrating community. Truly meaningful liturgy cannot be imposed on a community for the simple reason that the liturgy is meant to celebrate the Christian reality of *that* community. If the eucharist as a ritual is the intersection of the meaning of the Christ-mystery with the meaning of the lives of the gathered Christians, both of these meanings must be recognized by the people, explicitly stated, and allowed to interpret one another. The eucharist should express and celebrate the joys and sorrows, the hopes, dreams and problems, the needs and commitments of the gathered community. It must celebrate the hope that dreams can be realized, commitments can be honored, sorrow changed to joy because of the presence to their lives of the risen Lord. This is what lies behind the liturgical moment of the prayers of the faithful.

One of the most important ways the eucharist incorporates the life experience of the community is by *reconciliation*—which is always required for genuine community. Because humans, even the best of us, are not perfect, there are a variety of alienations that keep us divided from one another, that diminish and harm whole segments of our society. These alienations exist within the church itself. We have become more explicitly conscious of them in recent decades—racial and ethnic prejudice, sexism, homophobia, divisions between rich and poor, a generation gap—and we have realized how central they are in the systemic evil that destroys lives. Humanity needs to be healed from these alienations. This is a large part of what "salvation" is all about.

Alienation is not a new problem. Indeed, it is intrinsic to what we have traditionally called "original sin." Jesus' own mission and ministry were directed to reconciliation. The task of the church as it works with the risen Christ in healing the world is one of reconciliation. The Christian ministry of reconciliation is sacramental in the strict sense of that term, because it reveals the divine reconciling that takes place through it. The eucharist is the key ritual that simultaneously expresses and helps bring about this reconciling action of God in Christ. In actual practice the eucharist celebrated by a particular community ought to touch the need for reconciling within that community and in that portion of the world where the community resides.

Clearly the eucharist cannot function in this life-changing way unless it provides a situation in which people can share their life experiences. This is certainly much easier in smaller eucharistic groups, and it does happen in many "base communities." But even in these intimate gatherings effort and creativity are needed to make the ritual open to sharing. Larger parish celebrations can achieve a measure of sharing when parish leadership is alert to the human issues that dominate the interest and energy of the congregation. The homily plays a crucial role in linking the message of the gospel with the concrete demands of life. Homilies of this kind can occur only if the homilist is truly part, and *humanly* part, of the parish community.

The eucharist should not be an isolated moment of celebrating our Christianity. We need, within the family or similar groupings, to recover or initiate the practice of celebrating *as Christians* many of life's important events. In some ethnic groups it was customary to celebrate the anniversary of baptism. Similarly, confirmation could become more central in a young person's life if it were a major celebration within the family. There have been a number of creative suggestions for ways to link the ritual of weddings more closely to wedding receptions. These are only the more obvious instances; there are many other occasions when families and friends could ritualize in a Christian way the important things that have happened to them. As such liturgies become part of Catholics' lives, they would flow naturally into celebrations of the eucharist. Probably the most important part of such ritual extension of eucharist into the whole of life would be a recovery in the family of the rhythms of the liturgical year.

Eucharist and Discipleship

One of the underlying attitudes that is changing the reality of eucharist is an awakening to the challenge of discipleship that comes with it. Vatican II's assertion that the church is the entire people of God has given rise to the realization that active discipleship is both a right and a responsibility that comes with Christian baptism. At the same time we have become more aware that discipleship may well have its price. Dietrich Bonhoeffer's classic work *The Cost of Discipleship* detailed that price. The martyrdom of Archbishop Oscar Romero, the four American women working with the poor in El Salvador and the six men and women murdered at the Jesuit university in that country made it clear that following Christ can demand the ultimate price. Accepting discipleship in the eucharistic celebration may not be so dramatic, but it does demand some espousal of a counter-cultural outlook and way of life

One important aspect involved in the choice of discipleship is that it needs to be done *prayerfully*. Choice of discipleship is always a response to Christ's word of invitation: "Come, follow me." Responding to God's word is the essential element of Christian prayer, and it finds its prime example in the community's eucharistic "amen" to the call to be disciples in today's world. Eucharist, if it would transform people, must go beyond the recitation of formulated prayers and *pray* the liturgy.

To insist that the eucharist should be prayed in no way requires that the liturgy be characterized by a sort of artificial piety. Just the contrary. The celebration of eucharist should be a simple and straightforward "word" of the particular group that is gathered. It should be *natural* in the sense that people are not "wearing their prayer masks" but are the people they ordinarily are. This sounds obvious, yet most Catholics are only slowly learning to relax and be themselves at eucharist. Yet it is as *themselves* that they must be transformed by the ritual of the liturgy. At the same time, because eucharist is a special event marked by beauty and awe, it needs to be celebrated with care and by genuine involvement of people in the praying and singing. One aspect of effective eucharistic liturgy that is often overlooked is silence. If the people who are gathered are to respond in any depth to the message of the ritual, they must have a chance to steep themselves in it. A good homily can stimulate and guide our thinking, but only our own reflection can lead to insight and conversion. Liturgy cannot be rushed and have its effect. Liturgy is a celebration, and the pace of the ritual must allow people to enjoy it in relaxed fashion. This is particularly true of those major festive eucharists like the Easter Vigil or Pentecost that highlight the liturgical cycle.

Much of what we have said in this chapter about the manner of celebrating eucharistic liturgy is no news to many Catholics. It is what Catholics are now searching for, and sometimes finding, in their worship. The awareness of what eucharist can and should be and the desire to find eucharistic celebrations that fulfill this need is one of the major influences now driving liturgical change. That influence will increase as Catholics experience appropriate eucharistic liturgies more often, because nothing so instructs people about what eucharist can be as does the experience of what it really is. At work in all this is the Spirit of God—working often at depths scarcely noticed, but working in ways that are ultimately irresistible. For that reason, the future of eucharist is very promising.